· *For Michael, my Mother and my Father* ·

Longman Group Limited

Longman House, Burnt Mill, Harlow,
Essex CM20 2JE, England,
and Associated Companies throughout the World

A TEMPLAR BOOK
Devised and produced by Templar Publishing,
Old King's Head Court, Dorking, Surrey RH4 1AR

This edition first published 1986.
Originally published in 1871 as part of
'Nonsense Songs, Stories, Botany, and Alphabets'

Lear, Edward
[ABC]. Edward Lear's ABC: alphabet rhymes
for children
1. English language—Alphabet—Juvenile
literature
I. Title   II. Pike, Carol
421'.1   PE1155

ISBN 0-582-23624-X

Designed by Mick McCarthy
Origination by Positive Colour Ltd, Maldon, Essex
Printed by Tien Wah Press Ltd, Singapore

·EDWARD·LEAR'S·
ABC

·EDWARD·LEAR'S·
ABC

Alphabet rhymes for children

ILLUSTRATED BY
CAROL PIKE

Longman

A was once an apple pie,
Pidy, Widy
Tidy, Widy
Nice insidy
Apple Pie!

B was once a little bear,
Beary! Wary!
Hairy! Beary!
Taky cary!
Little Bear!

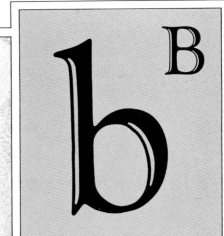

C was once a little cake,
Caky, Baky
Maky, Caky
Taky caky
Little Cake!

D was once a little doll,
  Dolly, Molly
  Polly, Nolly
  Nursy dolly
  Little Doll!

E e

E was once a little eel,
Eely, Weely
Peely, Eely
Twirly, Tweely
Little Eel!

F was once a little fish,
Fishy, Wishy
Squishy, Fishy
In a dishy
Little Fish!

f F

G g

G was once a little goose,
Goosy, Moosy
Boosey, Goosey
Waddle-woosy
Little Goose!

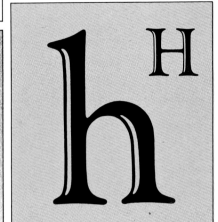

H was once a little hen,
Henny, Chenny
Tenny, Henny
Eggsy-any
Little Hen!

i I

I was once a bottle of ink,
Inky, Dinky
Thinky, Inky
Blacky minky
Bottle of Ink!

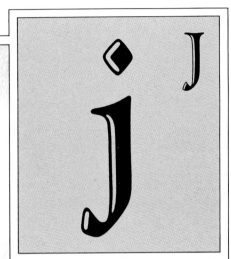

J was once a jar of jam,
Jammy, Mammy
Clammy, Jammy
Sweety-swammy
Jar of Jam!

K was once a little kite,
Kity, Whity
Flighty, Kity
Out of sighty–
Little Kite!

L was once a little lark,
Larky! Marky!
Harky! Larky!
In the parky
Little Lark!

1^L

M
m

M was once a little mouse,
Mousey, Bousey
Sousy, Mousy
In the housy
Little Mouse!

N was once a little needle,
Needly, Tweedly
Threedly, Needly
Wisky-wheedly
Little Needle!

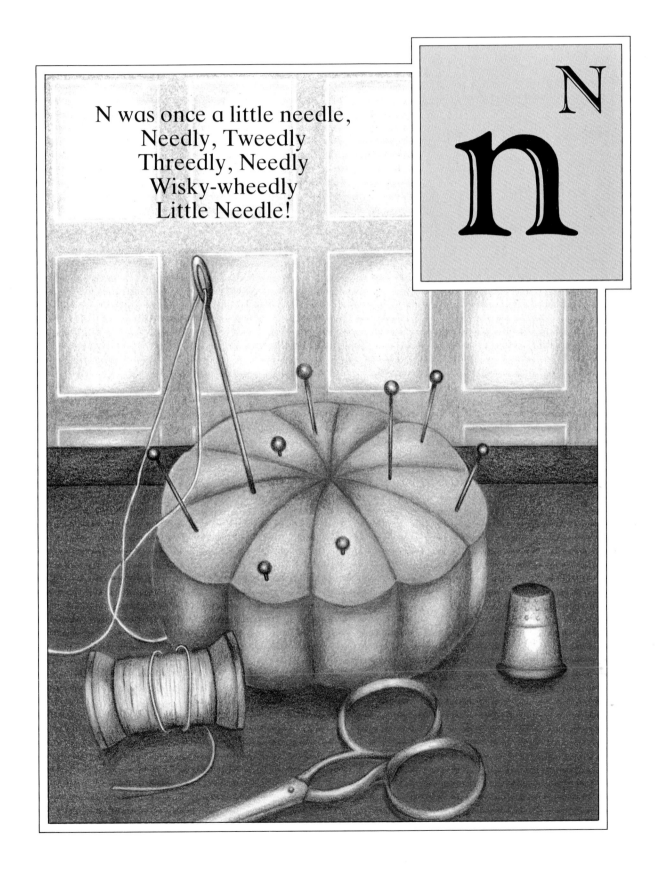

O was once a little owl,
Owly, Prowly
Howly, Owly
Browny-fowly
Little Owl!

P was once a little pump,
Pumpy, Slumpy
Flumpy, Pumpy
Dumpy, Thumpy
Little Pump!

P p

Q was once a little quail,
Quaily, Faily
Daily, Quaily
Stumpy-taily
Little Quail!

R was once a little rose,
Rosy, Posy
Nosy, Rosy
Blows-y – grows-y
Little Rose!

r R

S S

S was once a little shrimp,
Shrimpy, Nimpy
Flimpy, Shrimpy
Jumpy-jimpy
Little Shrimp!

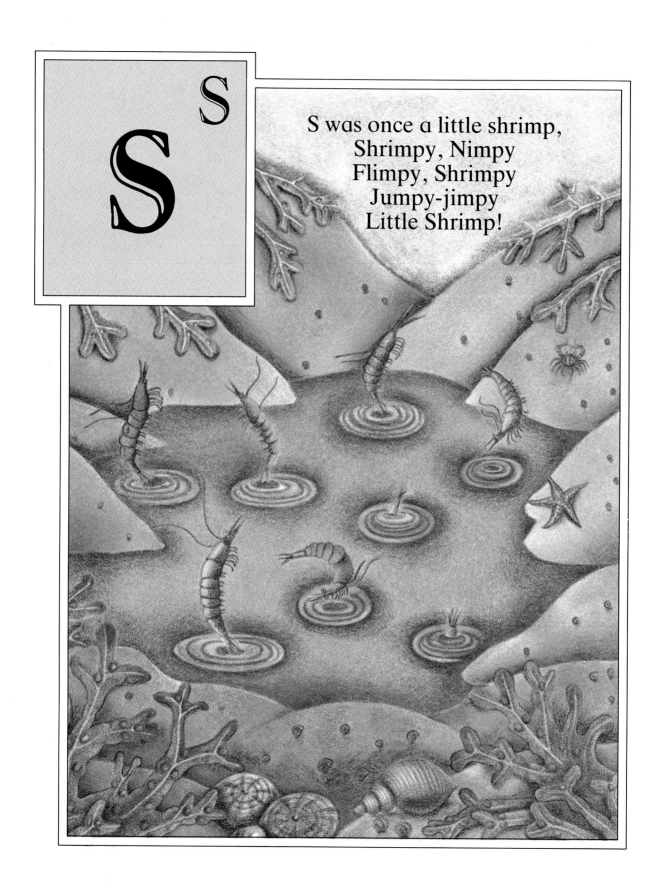

T was once a little thrush,
Thrushy! Hushy!
Bushy! Thrushy!
Flitty-flushy
Little Thrush!

t T

U
U

U was once a little urn,
Urny, Burny
Turny, Urny
Bubbly-burny
Little Urn!

V was once a little vine,
Viny, Winy
Twiny, Viny
Twisty-twiny
Little Vine!

V
v

W
W

W was once a whale,
Whaly, Scaly
Shaly, Whaly
Tumbly-taily
Mighty Whale!

X was once a great king Xerxes,
Xerxy, Perxy
Turxy, Xerxy
Linxy, Lurxy
Great King Xerxes!

Y

y

Y was once a little yew,
Yewdy, Fewdy
Crudy, Yewdy
Growdy, Grewdy
Little Yew!

Z was once a piece of zinc,
    Tinky, Winky
    Blinky, Tinky
    Tinkly, Minky
    Piece of Zinc!